KU KLUX KLAN

SECRETS EXPOSED

by

Ezra A. Cook

**Attitude toward Jews, Catholics, Foreigners
and Masons. Fraudulent
Methods Used. Atrocities
Committed in Name
of Order.**

ISBN-13:
978-1981593897

ISBN-10:
1981593896

CONTENTS

KU KLUX KLAN SECRETS EXPOSED

CHAPTER I

THE OLD KU KLUX KLAN

To the old Ku-Klux Klan which rode through the south in the days following the civil war the new Ku-Klux Klan is a relative only in name.

It is not tied by blood. It holds the same position to its southern aristocratic forbear as an imposter in social life does to some illustrious gentleman of the same name of whom he claims to be a descendant.

The old Ku-Klux Klan was a historical development. The new is a man's contrivance. The old Ku-Klux Klan movement was an outcome of conditions that prevailed in the southern states after the war. The present Klan, apparently, is an outcome of a group of men's desire to make money.

Widespread, spontaneous, popular, the movement of 1866 grew out of a disordered society, not as a "movement" at all at first, but as a scheme for having fun, a source of amusement among a group of young, full-blooded southern men to puzzle outsiders. Its use as a weapon against the stranger in the old south came later.

The "stranger" was the northern carpetbagger. To the south he was the pestilence that follows war. He was the blunderer who entered the land whose social customs were unknown to him, in a year when the fabric by those social customs was in need of mending.

NO RELIGIOUS TEST

When southern society seized the Ku-Klux Klan as an instrument with which to resist there were only two classes, carpet-bagger and unruly negro, against which it operated. To join the ranks of the white-robed horsemen, there were no qualifications of religion. The Klan made no mention of Jew or Catholic. Its purpose was to restore order, not to fan prejudice, and therein lies the difference between the old Klan and the present Klan which makes the latter a maverick.

The first unit of the horseback riding knights was founded in the village of Pulaski, Tenn., with the same motive for its organization as the old-time college hazing society. Its members were young men who had come back from the war, poor, exhausted, discouraged, and bored with the tameness of a country town.

HOW IT STARTED

According to the story which has lived south of the Mason and Dixon line since those post-bellum days, a group of youths cooling their heels in a law office one May evening in 1866 organized a society for a good time. If anyone had suggested to them at that time that five years later a committee of congress would devote thirteen volumes to a history of their "movement" and pass a law to suppress it, or that before the child of their wits was fully grown it would have developed into a terrorizing "hobgoblin" sheeted for lawlessness, they would have thought it a jest.

When their mere joke had become a grim joke, neighbors who feared it found in its name "Ku-Klux" the suggestion of a clicking rifle. But the name itself was proposed by its charter members in Tennessee as a derivative of the Greek word "Kuklos," meaning a circle. From "Kuklos" to "Ku-Klux" was an easy transition. The "Klan" followed because these youthful students of Greek had an ear for the alliterative.

From the Pulaski law office the society migrated to a haunted house on the outskirts of the village. Its members found their first source of amusement in initiation rites. They named their chief officer a Grand Cyclops and their vice president a Grand Magi. Other officers were the Grand Turk, or marshal; a Grand Exchequer or treasurer, and two Lictors.

WORE WHITE MASKS

The only germ in their constitution from which the "Imperial Wizard" Simmons of the twentieth century Klan could breed his present organization was the promise of absolute secrecy. For his copying years later, the first Klan also contrived a disguise. It consisted of a white mask, a tall cardboard hat, a gown or robe, and for the night riding excursions, a cover for the horses' bodies and mufflers for their feet.

Only after the Pulaski organization had entertained itself for many nights did the phenomenon present itself which was to make the Klan a weapon in the progress of post-war reconstruction. It was the discovery that the African negro was twice as fearful of mysticism and mystery as the white man. It taught the white men of Tennessee and neighboring states that they had a means of their own of preventing what they considered political mismanagement and social insolence in the control by northerners and freedmen of the state government.

BECOMES MILITARY ORGANIZATION

The Pulaski riders made themselves popular. Young men of neighboring towns organized brother Klans. When southern society found itself a Humpty Dumpty fallen from the wall, it grasped the Pulaski idea as the means for pulling itself up again. The Klan became a military organization, with the purpose of keeping order among the [8]negroes by intimidating them. Mysticism in the order grew. Humor grew with it, and by the time the states of the north discovered that the south had an organization which was in purpose a society of regulators, the young southern war veterans were donning their white robes and cardboard hats with a human skull and two thigh bones as the symbols of allegiance.

The oath which the grand cyclops administered has been preserved in southern diaries and documents. It was taken in a solemn manner as the knights were grouped amid the bones. The oath follows.

"We (or I, as the case might be) do solemnly swear before Almighty God and these witnesses, and looking upon these human bones, that I will obey and carry into effect every order made by any cyclops or assistant cyclops, and if I fail strictly to conform and execute every order made, as above required of me, unless I am prevented from some cause which shall be no fault of mine, or if I shall give any information to any person or persons except members of this order, that the doom of all traitors shall be meted out to me, and that my bones may become as naked and dry as the bones I am looking upon. And I take this oath voluntarily, without any mental reservation or evasion whatever, for the causes set out in said order, so help me God."

Ku-Klux horsemen who rode white-sheeted through the south in the nights of 1866 regarded themselves as upholders of sectional patriotism.

They considered themselves the spiritual descendants of the New Englanders who threw the English tea overboard into Boston harbor nearly 100 years before. Their protests, and the acts of intimidation by which they enforced their protests were against the white "carpetbagger" from the north, the negro freedman to whom liberty meant arrogant office-holding, and the "scalawag," by which terms they designated those deserters from the southern aristocracy who had joined the ranks of the northern stranger.

The second stage came within a year after the secret body had its birth, when the band of burlesquers became a band of regulators.

To the south, the reconstruction acts which congress passed in 1867 were pernicious. The one-time white confederate soldier believed that the congressional legislation made official mismanagement permanent. He saw negroes organized into the militia. He saw his former slaves voting twice and thrice at elections where he himself had to pass, literally, under bayonets to reach the polls. He disliked the freedman's bureau, which substituted northern alien machinery for the old patriarchal relation between white employer and black employe. He heard drunken negroes at his gates in the night. He saw the "carpetbagger" urging upon the freedman civic rights which he knew the latter was not educated enough to perform.

FIRST OBJECTS POLITICAL

These were the prejudices against which the original Ku-Klux Klan threw itself. They were surface indications of an historical development. They had nothing to do with the racial and religious biases which the present Klan attempted to propagate. To the present Klan, the old Klan, in its first stage, was unrelated. In its second stage it was related only in its methods of terrorism and its removal of justice from the courts to the masques until its own leaders were powerless to check it.

The Klan early fell a victim to the abuses inseparable from secrecy. It happened that Tennessee, the birthplace of the hooded institution, was also the first southern state to find itself turned upside down in reconstruction. "Dem Ku-Kluxes," as the negro called the mysterious union, became a band of regulators. Their first official convention was held in Nashville early in 1867.

The Klan, which, until then, had been bound together only by the deference which priority rights gave to the grand cyclops of the parental Pulaski "den," was organized into the "Invisible Empire of the South." It was ruled by a grand wizard of the whole empire, a grand dragon of each realm, or state, a grand titan of each dominion, or [10]county, a grand cyclops of each den, and staff officers with names as equally suggestive of Arabian Nights.

LAWS DEFINE OBJECTS

For the first time its laws defined serious objects. First was the duty of protecting people, presumably white southerners, from indignities and wrongs; second was the duty of succoring the suffering, particularly among the families of dead confederate soldiers; finally was the oath to defend "the constitution of the United States and all laws passed in conformity thereto," and of the states also, to aid in executing all constitutional laws, and to protect the people from unlawful seizures and from trial otherwise than by jury.

It is these purposes which Imperial Wizard Simmons of the modern clan pretends to perpetuate, plus persecutions of Jews, Catholics and negroes, while denying charges of terrorizing outbreaks.

The Nashville convention chose Gen. Nathan B. Forrest, the confederate cavalry leader, as its supreme ruler. He is known to have increased the membership of the hooded horsemen in the old south to 550,000. Among his aides were Generals John B. Gordon, A.H. Colquitt, G.T. Anderson, A.B. Lawton, W.J. Hardee, John C. Brown, George W. Gordon and Albert Pike. The latter became one of the foremost authorities of Masonry.

Terrorism spread, until during the political campaign which preceded the 1868 presidential election, 2,000 persons were killed and injured in Louisiana by Ku-Klux Klansmen, who rode at night, disguised as freebooters, and according to James G. Blaine, defeated candidate for the presidency at a later date, hesitated at no cruelty.

In the north, in the years immediately after the civil war, the original Ku-Klux Klan was called a conspiracy.

In the south, where society was being ground in the mills of reconstruction, the Klan started its midnight rovings as an instrument of moral force. But within three years its [11]period of usefulness, as the white southerner saw it useful, was over.

Its founders had played with it as with an exciting bonfire. During the months, however, when former confederate soldiers used it to frighten away northern officeholders with oppressive tactics, it had leaped in size until when the moment came for smothering it out its leaders discovered it beyond control.

Not until the full fire department of federal and state law had been called out did the Invisible Empire cease to operate.

TENNESSEE ACTS AGAINST IT

By 1872 the white-robed knights of midnight, whose purpose to enforce law had in itself yielded to lawlessness, were for the most part disappeared. But so, in one state after another, had the northern carpetbagger and the southern scalawag.

Tennessee, where the Klan was founded, was the first to take legislative action against it. In September, 1868, its legislature passed a statute making membership in the Klan punishable by a fine of $500 and imprisonment for not less than five years.

As a result, in February, 1869, Gen. Nathan B. Forrest, former cavalry officer of the confederate army, who was grand wizard of the order, officially proclaimed the Ku-Klux Klan and Invisible Empire dissolved and disbanded forever.

But members of the adventurous law-assuming organization were reluctant to yield their mysterious power.

The wizard's order went into effect. Klan property was burned.

NEW BANDS SPRING UP

But immediately in southern states, as far west as Arkansas, there sprang up disguised bands, some of them [12]neighborhood groups only, some of them bands of ruffians who traveled in the night to win personal ends, still others new orders founded in imitation of the Ku-Klux and using similar methods.

Of the last, the Knights of the White Camellia was the largest. In some private notebooks of the south its membership was said to be even larger than the parent Klan.

From New Orleans early in 1868, it spread across to Texas and back to the Carolinas. Racial supremacy was its purpose.

Only white men 18 years or older were invited to the secrets of its initiation, and in their oath they promised not only to be obedient and secret, but to "maintain and defend the social and political superiority of the white race on this continent."

Initiates were enjoined, notwithstanding, to show fairness to the negroes and to concede to them in the fullest measure "those rights which we recognize as theirs."

"PALE FACES" AND OTHERS

Other bands of nightriders responded to the names of "Pale Faces," "White Leaguers," the "White Brotherhood" and the "Constitutional Union Guards."

Surviving members are hazy as to their aims and methods, the character of their membership, their members, and the connection between them.

Federal recognition that the Invisible Empire, whether it was the original Klan or not, was everywhere a real empire came in the spring of 1871, when a senate committee presented majority and minority reports on the result of its investigations of the white man's will to rule against the freedmen's militia in the south.

The majority report found that the Ku-Klux Klan was a criminal conspiracy of a distinctly political nature against the laws and against the colored citizens.

The minority found that Ku-Klux disorder and violence was due to misgovernment and an exploitation of the states below the Mason and Dixon line by radicals.

CONGRESS ACTS AGAINST KLAN

The first Ku-Klux bill was passed in April, 1871, "to enforce the fourteenth amendment." Power of the president to use troops to put down the white-hooded riders was hinted at.

In the next month the second Ku-Klux bill was passed to enforce "the right of citizens in the United States to vote."

In 1872 federal troops were sent into the south to back up his anti-Ku-Klux proclamation. By the end of 1872 the "conspiracy" was thought to be overthrown.

At various times individuals in the south and elsewhere have tried to put breath into the Klan's dead body.

It was left for "Grand Wizard" Simmons of Atlanta to accomplish it. His new organization, he explains, is imbued with the Ku-Klux "spirit."

"That this spirit may live always to warm the hearts of many men," he says, "is the paramount ideal of the Knights of the Ku-Klux Klan."

President Grant answered: "Thou shalt not" to the Ku-Klux Klan in 1871. He backed up his word with armed troops.

During the whole of one session of congress senators and representatives serving in Washington in the years just after the civil war occupied themselves in stripping the masques off the southern night-riders.

Into the country south of the Mason and Dixon line they dispatched congressional investigators, whose duty it was to enter the "portals of the invisible empire" and discover what was hiding behind them. When they reported that the Ku-Klux Klan, decked out in the uniform of ghosts, was waging midnight warfare on the negro and carpet-bagger congress passed legislation which suppressed the order.

PUTS ROBES OUT OF FASHION

Action was quick. Almost before the government printing presses had finished turning out ten volumes in which [14]the committee recorded the results of their investigation the white robes and hoods of the Ku-Kluxes had gone out of fashion in the old south.

President Grant in 1871 was without precedent. His law enforcers, just getting acquainted with the amendment which freed the slaves, were without a statute to deal with the armed clique which proposed to keep the negro down in the day by frightening him in the night. The emergency bill which congress passed at that period empowers the regular army or the navy to put down any unlawful combination which is doing domestic violence.

When congress met for its forty-second session in 1871, the cross bones and skull and coffin with which the Ku-Klux were marking their threats had become the symbols of terrorism in the south. So grave was the situation that speakers on the floor of the house, when the session opened, classed the conspiracy of the Klan "less formidable, but not less dangerous to American liberty" than the just-ended war of the rebellion. They charged that as well as binding its members to execute crimes against its opponents in the social-political life of the south, it protected them against conviction and punishment by perjury on the witness stand and in the jury box. Representatives asked why, of all offenders, not one had been convicted.

PRESIDENT URGES ACTION

On March 23, 1871, President Grant sent a message to both houses in which he recommended that all other business be postponed until the Klan was made subservient to the flag.

"A condition of affairs now exists in some of the states of the Union rendering life and property insecure and the carrying of the mails and the collection of revenue dangerous," his message said. "The proof that such a condition of affairs exists in some localities is now before the senate. That the power to correct these evils is beyond the control of the senate authorities I do not doubt; that the power of the executive of the United States, acting within the limits [15]of existing laws is sufficient for present emergencies, is not clear. Therefore, I urgently recommend such legislation as in the judgment of congress shall effectually secure, life, liberty and property and the enforcement of law in all parts of the United States. It may be expedient to provide that such law as shall be passed in pursuance of this recommendation shall expire at the end of the next session of congress. There is no other subject on which I would recommend legislation during the present session."

"FORCE BILL AT DISPOSAL"

The law which was at the disposal of President Harding was popularly known as "the Force bill." Under congressional passage it was entitled "An act to enforce the Fourteenth amendment of the constitution of the United States and for other purposes." President Grant approved it April 20, 1871.

It is aimed at two or more persons who conspire to use force and intimidation "outside the law." It forbids them to go in disguise along a public highway or upon the premises of another person for the purpose, either directly or indirectly, of depriving that person of equal privileges under the law. Punishment for the offense may be imprisonment from six months to six years, a fine not less than $500, nor more than $5,000, or both.

The act took particular action against the practice of the Klanists of protecting each other in court. It provides that every man called for service on a jury in a Klan case shall take oath in open court that he is not a member of nor has ever aided or advised any such "unlawful, combination or conspiracy."

DISGUISE IS BARRED

That individual was declared a violator of the law who shall "go in disguise upon the public highway or upon the [16]premises of another for the purpose, either directly or indirectly, of depriving any person or class of persons of the equal protection of the laws, or of equal privileges or immunities under the laws, or by force, intimidation or threat to prevent any citizen lawfully entitled to vote from giving his support or advocacy in a lawful manner toward the election of any lawfully qualified person for office."

The act states further: "That in all cases where insurrection, domestic violence, unlawful combinations or conspiracies in any state shall so obstruct or hinder the execution of the laws thereof, and of the United States, as to deprive any portion or class of the people of any rights, privileges or immunities or protection, and the constituted authorities of such state shall either be unable to protect, or shall fail in or refuse protection, it shall be unlawful for the president, and it shall be his duty, to take such measures by the employment of the militia or the land and naval forces of the United States for the suppression of such insurrection."

"KU-KLUX" FILLS RECORDS

Pages of the Congressional Globe, as the present Congressional Record was then called, were filled during the months before the passage of this act with the word "Ku-Klux."

The verb "Kukluxed" became in the mouths of senators and representatives arguing over the bill a synonym for "intimidated." Friends of the nightriders termed them "modern knights of the Round Table," and "conservators of law and order." Opponents on the floor of the house advocated a policy of "amnesty for every rebel, hanging for every Ku-Klux."

Black and white victims of the gun-toting ghosts were brought from Tennessee, Georgia, Louisiana, Texas and other states where the Klan rode to recount before the congressional committee the details of their persecutions. Their accounts as the government documents preserve [17]them might well have been a primer, it has been said, for the acts of later Lenines and Trotzkys.

REPORT OF OFFENSES VARIES

The report of the congressional committee is a recital varying from mirth to murder. In one county the victim of the hooded Klan might be an itinerant minister who had offended by teaching a negro mammy to pray. Next door a Ku-Klux sign, with a coffin painted in blood, might be hung over the dead body of a "bad" negro whose freedom had made him officious.

One negro was whipped for stealing a beef. Another was tarred and feathered because his daughter ran away from the white man who had employed her.

Colored cooks were beaten for talking saucily to their southern mistresses. Northern white women were threatened for hiring colored cooks.

IGNORES NOTE, DIES

When a negro ignored a note carrying the Ku-Klux skull and cross bones and voted "republican" instead of "conservative," his body, ornamented with skull and bones in blood, might be found the next morning in the middle of the road—lifeless.

The congressional minutes report a bold, public display of the Klan's official orders. They might appear in a whisk of the wind on the post office window. They might be pinned on a tree or pole or building. On one occasion, when a member of the Klan was on trial in a county court, a band of white masquers, riding through the courtyard on horse, dropped a note addressed to the court, grand jury and sheriff.

"Go slow," it commanded. At the bottom was a drawing of a coffin and on each side a rope. The signature was "K.K.K."

[18]Ku-Klux rule in the south half a century ago was an attempt to govern by masque.

Secret covenants arrived at by a sheeted brotherhood, veiled signs, orders written in blood and posted at midnight on the victim's door—by such means did the Klan substitute the masque for the ballot.

Congressional investigating committees who stripped the night-riding organization of secrecy during the administration of President Grant, were entertained during a session of congress by tales of lares and lemures howling at night in fields or on crossroads, bad luck omens for the negroes.

UNDER MARTIAL LAW

In organization the Klan was military, and its town, county and state rule, as recorded in the Congressional Globe, operated as under martial law.

As the revolt of the white southerner to colored and northern domination reared itself into giant-size, towns under Klan domination came to take their rule and law from the K.K.K. note, flapping in the wind on a tree or fencepost, with the coffin on its signature, urging that it be obeyed.

WARN CARPET BAGGERS

In South Carolina, according to the report of the federal committee, townsfolk journeyed to the postoffice, not to get their mail, but to read the daily Ku-Klux bulletin. One such, reprinted in the ten-volume report of the committee which examined southern outrages, was a warning against further "carpet bagger" administration. It is as follows:

Headquarters, Ninth Division, S.C.
Special Orders, No. 3, K.K.K.

Ignorance is the curse of God.

For that reason we are determined that members of the [19]legislature, the school committee and the county commissioners of Union county shall no longer officiate.

Fifteen days' notice from this date is given, and if they, and all, do not at once and forever resign their present inhuman, disgraceful and outrageous rule, then retributive justice will as surely be used as night follows day.

By order of the Grand Chief,
A.O., Grand Secretary.

THREATEN NEGROES FOR FIRES

Another "special order," this one warning that the colored race in general would be punished for all malicious fires in particular, was made public in the Charleston News, Jan. 31, 1871.

Headquarters, K.K.K.
January 22, 1871.

Resolved: That in all cases of incendiarism, ten of the leading colored people and two white sympathizers shall be executed.

That if any armed bands of colored people are found hereafter picketing the roads, the officers of the company to which the pickets belong shall be executed.

Southern speakers on the floor of the house in the debates which preceded the passage of the "act to enforce the fourteenth amendment," traced the origin of the Ku-Klux to the Union league, an association in the south composed chiefly of northerners. Charges were also made by statesmen once in the confederate army that "Tammany Hall" in New York furnished arms to the Klanists, in order that they might murder southern republicans.

SUPPRESSED IN 1871

When the act suppressing the Klan was approved by President Grant on April 20, 1871, it was estimated that the night riders were operating in eleven states of the south. Six months later, in October, President Grant [20]issued a proclamation calling on members of illegal associations in nine counties in South Carolina to disperse and surrender their arms and disguises in five days.

Five days afterwards, another proclamation was issued suspending the privileges of the writ of habeas corpus in the counties named. More than 200 persons were arrested within a few days. It is believed that the Ku-Klux Klan was practically overthrown by the middle of the following January.

CHAPTER II

THE NEW KU KLUX KLAN

Must Every Citizen be a Slave of Fear Spread by Masked Night-Riders, or Will He Live under the Protection of the Constitution of the United States?

Are you a citizen of the United States? If you are it is to your interest to inform yourself about the Ku-Klux Klan. As a citizen you are under the protection of the constitution of the United States. The Ku Klux Klan has set itself above the constitution. It has made laws of its own. Its members have inaugurated a reign of lawlessness that may drag you out of your bed at midnight and submit you to a coat of tar and feathers through the whims of some neighbor who does not like the country in which you were born, or who objects to your religion, your color, your opinions, your personal habits or anything else about you that does not suit his fancy.

The constitution guarantees that your house, your person and your papers and effects are free from unlawful search and seizure; that you cannot be deprived of life, liberty or property without due process of law, which law must be publicly enforced in God's sunshine by persons legally chosen; that when you are accused of any delinquency or crime you shall have a speedy, public trial before a judge and an impartial jury; that you may be a member of any religious denomination or sect with whom you may worship as you please; that you have the right of free speech; that you cannot be held in involuntary servitude except as a punishment for crime, for which you have been found guilty in a legal way; that you cannot be denied the right to vote on account of your color.

MASKED MEN DEFY CONSTITUTION

Masked riders of the night disagree with these guarantees of freedom. They break into your house under cover of darkness unlawfully seize your person and ride away with you, depriving you of liberty without due process of law. They accuse you of charges that may or may not be true, without giving you the opportunity of knowing the identity of your accusers, because they are masked. They try you without giving you a chance to defend yourself. They make themselves accuser, judge, jury and executioner. They deny that you have the right to worship God as you please. They deny your right to free speech, because they forbid you to criticise what they do.

The Ku Klux Klan clamps involuntary servitude on its own members by making them take oaths to uphold their leaders, even when they violate the constitution. It aims to place those whom it opposes under its heel. It openly defies the article of the constitution that guarantees race equality, by binding its members to put the black race under the supremacy of the white.

The American constitution says that if you were born abroad, but have become a naturalized citizen of the United States, you have as many rights here as though you were actually born here. The Ku Klux Klan is against the constitution on that point. The Ku Klux Klan wants to make the foreigner a serf.

The Ku Klux Klan has set itself up as a regulator of morals. Persons against whom there has been neighborhood gossip have been tarred and feathered. Thanks to the *New York World*, court records have been published showing that some of the highest persons in the Ku Klux have been involved in proceedings as disgraceful as those for which tar and feather parties have been organized by the Klan or persons masquerading as Ku Klux.

MISTREAT WHITES AND BLACKS

Men and women, white and black—have been mistreated by masked men. The number of these attacks grows as the [23]Klan increases in size. At present the Klan has branches in all states of the union except three—New Hampshire, Montana and Utah. In each state the law would be enforced by legal officials against any persons guilty of crime if public spirited citizens would make it their business to assist public officials to round up law breakers. The Klan, however, believes in its own method of punishment against those whom it opposes. It protects its own members and there is no case on record where a Klansman has been outraged. The Klan has one law for itself and another for its victims. The revelations of scandal among its leaders have not resulted in any movement on the part of its members to "clean house." Its motto seems to be "A Klansman can do no wrong." The lesson to be drawn from the revelations is that those in high places in the Klan have played on the gullibility of tens of thousands of otherwise sensible Americans. These leaders have become rich by dealing in the hocuspocus of mysticism, secret rites and high sounding phrases and by inflaming the passions of dupes by false stories involving religions and races.

In the south they have preached and conspired against the negroes. This hatred also has been carried into certain sections of large cities of the north where there are large negro populations. In some states they have played upon the feelings of those who might be drawn into the Klan by a crusade against Catholics. They have made use of counterfeit documents in secret bids for membership on this score. In cities like New York and Chicago, where the populations are largely Jewish, they have fanned the flames of religious hatred by propaganda against the Jews. Where foreign-born residents are living in large numbers the Klan has secretly intrigued against them. On the Pacific coast this propaganda is made against the Japanese; on the eastern seaboard it has been against persons born in European and Asiatic countries.

A GOLD MINE FOR PROMOTERS

Those who have investigated the Klan are convinced that its principal promoters are not inspired by a zeal for the welfare of the United States, but on the other hand they are certain that the promoters are in the Ku Klux Klan business to make money out of it; that they have profited by millions of dollars and that for this filthy money they have spread loose seeds of discontent and disorder that must be raked out of the body politic by the united action of all patriotic organizations and individuals. As far as its chief protagonists are concerned the Ku Klux is a huge money-making hoax—a gold mine. The poor dupes who have been "soaked" for regalia and dues will wake up some time and discover how they have been deluded and misled. In the meantime, however, it is the duty of every true American to inform himself about the Klan so that in whatever way may come to his lot he may counteract the terrible consequences of its teachings and practices.

CHAPTER III

HOW THE MODERN KU KLUX KLAN WAS ORGANIZED

Something about those who sit in judgment on the affairs of the "Invisible Empire"; their troubles in court.

William J. Simmons (who carries a bogus title as "colonel") is the "Imperial Wizard" of the "Invisible Empire, Knights of the Ku Klux Klan." He organized the masked men on Thanksgiving night in 1915. Some of the organizers associated with him had belonged to the original Ku Klux Klan which rampaged in the southern states after the Civil War, killing hundreds of negroes and whites, and which was put out of business by President U.S. Grant after the states had failed to do so.

Simmons and thirty-four others secured a charter from the state of Georgia on December 4, 1915. It is signed by Philip Cook, who was then secretary of state of that commonwealth. Later, on July 1, 1916, a special charter was issued by the Supreme court of Fulton county, Ga. The granting of the charters followed the organization of the Klan which occurred with midnight ceremonies on the top of Stone mountain, near Atlanta, Thanksgiving night.

THAT COLD WINTER NIGHT

In referring to the first ceremonies, Simmons has written as follows in the official records of the Ku Klux:

"On Thanksgiving night, 1915, men were seen emerging from the shadows and gathering round the spring at the base of Stone mountain, the world's greatest rock, near [26]Atlanta, Ga., and from thence repaired to the mountain top, and there under a blazing fiery cross they took the oath of allegiance to the Invisible Empire, Knights of the Ku Klux Klan.

"And thus on the mountain top that night at the midnight hour, while men braved the surging blasts of wild wintry mountain winds and endured a temperature far below freezing, bathed in the sacred glow of the fiery cross, the Invisible Empire was called from its slumber of half a century to take up a new task and fulfill a new mission for humanity's good, and to call back to mortal habitation the good angel of practical fraternity among men."

It will be noticed that Simmons refers to "a temperature far below freezing." The official weather reports of the region for that night show that the temperature was thirty degrees above the freezing point.

Simmons had a fraternal order in mind when he organized the Ku Klux. He had been an itinerant Methodist preacher and organizer for the Modern Woodmen of the World and had not met with success in either capacity. He was a good talker but lacked the "punch" to put things over. The Ku Klux Klan did not prosper under his direction. Then he met Edward Y. Clarke and Mrs. Elizabeth Tyler. Clarke and Mrs. Tyler were the owners of the Southern Publicity Association of Atlanta. During the war they had been publicity agents for various "drives," managed for the Y.M.C.A., such Y.W.C.A., the Salvation Army and such enterprises. Clarke saw the value of the publicity that could be coined from the old name of the Ku

Klux Klan and entered into an arrangement with Simmons to promote the Klan. He agreed to give Simmons $100 a week if Simmons would follow his directions. Simmons was to brush up on delivering speeches and writing articles for *The Searchlight*, a magazine which Clarke founded as the official organ of the Ku Klux.

From this joining of forces Simmons, Clarke and Mrs. Tyler have become rich. The Klan has extended its membership to all except three states and it claims that 500,000 to 700,000 Klansmen are in its ranks. Clarke is the [27]"Imperial Kleagle," or boss salesman of memberships. Mrs. Tyler is Grand Chief of Staff in charge of the woman's division of the Klan.

WHAT POLICE RECORDS SHOW

Investigation of the police and court records of Atlanta disclosed that Clarke and Mrs. Tyler were arrested in their night clothes in a house that Mrs. Tyler owned at No. 185 South Pryor street, Atlanta. This occurred in October, 1919. Clarke gave the name of "Jim Slaton" and Mrs. Tyler gave the name of "Mrs. Elizabeth Carroll."

The cases were on the book of the Recorder's court as City of Atlanta versus E.Y. Clarke and City of Atlanta versus Mrs. Elizabeth Tyler, page 305 of the docket of 1919, case numbers 17,005 and 17,006. The police were put on the trail of Clarke and Mrs. Tyler by Clarke's wife.

In addition to the charge of disorderly conduct, a charge of possessing whisky illegally was placed against Mrs. Tyler and Clarke. This was an amazing charge against Clarke because he had been known as one of the leaders of the anti-saloon movement in Georgia. The whisky charge was dropped when J.Q. Jett, son-in-law of Mrs. Tyler, claimed ownership of the whisky and was fined $25.

The Klan is supposed to stand for respect of women and children. The records of the Atlanta courts still contain charges against Clarke that he deserted and abandoned his wife and child. He never has denied the charges. Mrs. Clarke went to work to support herself and her little son. A suit for divorce was filed in October, 1919, by Mrs. Clarke, who charged that her husband had deserted her three years previously. After his arrest with Mrs. Tyler Clarke agreed to pay his wife $75 a month. Since Clarke has become prosperous in the Ku Klux Klan he has bought his wife a $10,000 house.

RECORDS ARE STOLEN

When newspaper men began to investigate Mrs. Tyler and Clarke, they discovered that the official records of the Atlanta police department and the Recorder's office had been mutilated. Somebody had stolen the pages from the books containing the records of the cases. Members of the Ku Klux Klan are numbered among the police and official attaches of the city and newspaper comment indicates that they helped smother the case in behalf of their leaders.

SCANDAL OF "CHAPLAIN" RIDLEY

Another leader of the Ku Klux Klan is "Rev." Caleb A. Ridley, who is the "Imperial Chaplain" of the order. He is a right-hand assistant of Mrs. Tyler and helps her to edit *The Searchlight*.

Ridley also has had an experience in the recorder's court. He was arrested on complaint of the husband of Mrs. J.B. Hamilton, who lives on Cooper street, Atlanta, not a great distance from the Central Baptist church, where Ridley preaches. Recorder Johnson dismissed the case against Ridley.

Mrs. Hamilton testified that Ridley used to walk past her house when she sat on the porch and smile up at her. One day, without being invited and with no encouragement from her, he walked up on the porch and sat next to her on a swing. She said he chatted with her about church questions, although she was not a member of his church. Then he placed his arm around her, tried to embrace her and said something that she thought was not proper.

One witness testified that he had seen Ridley go on the porch and sit on the swing. He had seen Mrs. Hamilton push Ridley away from her.

Ridley was supported by his flock. Several women testified in behalf of his character. He said he visited Mrs. Hamilton because she looked lonely.

CHAPTER IV

HOW THE KU KLUX KLAN GETS MEMBERS

First Approached by Mysterious Notes, the Candidate is Soaked for a "Donation" and Money for His Robes.

The man who is invited to join the Ku Klux Klan is kidded into the belief that he is one of the chosen of God's beings and that he is being honored because his presence in the ranks is an honor to himself as well as to the Klan. A kleagle is a common salesman. He has charge of a small district. He works under a king kleagle, who has charge of a state. He is the state salesmanager. A cyclops is in charge of the king kleagles and the kleagles in several states.

Here is the way one group of kleagles work. They are given the name of a person who is eligible. One kleagle is assigned to catch him. The kleagle sends the sucker the following message:

"Sir (or Brother)—Six thousand men who are preparing for eventualities have their eyes on you. You are being weighed in the balance!

"The Call is coming! Are you able and qualified to respond?

"Discuss this matter with no one."

"Yu-Bu-Tu"

A few days later this card is sent:

"Sir—You have heard from us because we believe in you. We are for you and Need you!

"The impenetrable Veil of Mystery is drawing aside. Soon you will appear exactly as you are.

"Are you a Real Man?

"Lift your eyes to the Fiery Cross and falter not, but go forward to the Light.

"Discuss this matter with no one.

"Yu-Bu-Tu"

After another short wait this third message is sent:

"Sir:

"You have been weighed in the balance and found Not wanting!

"Strong Men—Brave Men—R-e-a-l Men. We need such Men. We know you are one.

"The Goblins of the Invisible Empire will shortly issue their Call. Be discreet, preserve silence and bide its coming.

"Discuss this matter with no one.

"Yu-Bu-Tu"

By this time the candidate is supposed to be in a mood to fall, and the kleagle calls on him personally.

QUESTIONS FOR THE CANDIDATE

The kleagle presents the prospective initiate with the following list of questions to be answered:

(Note the questions marked with stars. They are used to bar out Jews, Catholics, negroes and foreign born.)

1. Is the motive prompting your inquiry serious?
2. What is you age?
3. What is your occupation?
4. Where where you born?
5. How long have you resided in your present locality?
6. Are you married, single or widower?
*7. Were your parents born in the United States of America?
*8. Are you a gentile or Jew?
*9. Are you of the white race or of a colored race?
10. What educational advantages have you?
11. Color of eyes? Hair? Weight? Height?
*12. Do you believe in the principles of Pure Americanism?
*13. Do you believe in white supremacy?
14. What is your politics?
*15. What is your religious faith?
*16. Of what church are you a member (if any)?
*17. Of what religious faith are your parents?
18. What secret, fraternal orders are you a member of (if any)?
19. Do you honestly believe in the practice of Real fraternity?
*20. Do you owe any kind of allegiance to any foreign nation, government, institution, sect, people, ruler or person?

I most solemnly assert and affirm that each question above is truthfully answered by me and in my own handwriting and that below is my real signature.
Signed ....
Inquirer.
       Business Address ....
       Telephone No. ....

Date .... 19..
Residence Address ....
Telephone No. ....

N.B.—If space above is not sufficient to answer questions,
then make your answer on the other side of this sheet. Number
the answer to correspond with the question.

If the candidate answers the question satisfactorily, he must pay his initiation fees, called "donation" and provide money to pay for his mask, robe, etc. This will be explained later. With his money affairs settled, he is ready for the initiation, together with whatever other candidates there are in the vicinity. The initiation services are held at midnight, with a flaming cross, an American flag, a sword or dagger, and a Bible as the chief outward signs of the order. There is also a bottle of water on the "altar."

CHAPTER V

OATH OF KU KLUX KLAN

Those who join the order must pledge blind allegiance to Constitution. They do not see.

Blind and unconditional obedience to the "constitution, laws, regulations usages and requirements" of the Ku Klux Klan, even to the extent of indorsing the principle of secret mob violence, is accepted by every person who takes the oath of Grand Wizard Simmons' Invisible Empire.

That every Klansman, under penalty of death, also agrees to carry out the mandates, degrees, edicts, rulings and "instructions" of Emperor Simmons also is shown in a reproduction of the oath as supplied by Klan organizers and officials.

The first section of this oath that carries veiled hints of violence to back it binds the members to unconditional obedience to a constitution he has never seen. Not only that but it binds him to obey any laws that may be enacted in the future, whether or not he approves of them. When he takes this obligation he gives a lease on his life to Simmons.

SWEARS TO ABSOLUTE SECRECY

Absolute secrecy even in the face of death is his second obligation and he promises that he "will pay promptly all just and legal demands made upon me to defray the expenses of my Klan when same are due or called for."

Then, with his left hand over his heart and his right hand raised to heaven and with the promise that "this oath I will seal with my blood," the candidate takes oath that he [33]"will most zealously and valiantly shield and preserve by any and all JUSTIFIABLE means and methods (not legal means and methods) the sacred constitutional rights and privileges of free public schools, free speech, free press, separation of church and state, liberty, white supremacy, just laws and the pursuit of happiness, against any encroachment of any nature by any person or persons, political party or parties, religious sect or people, native, naturalized or foreign, of any race, color, creed, lineage or tongue whatsoever."

MYSTERY IN AUTHORITY

Who defines the permissible limits of zeal and valor is not stated. Neither is it stated who decides when schools are free, speech and press free, nor when church and state are sufficiently separated. It is not stated whether it is the individual Klansman, the local Klan, the supreme council or the Imperial Wizard.

It has been revealed, however, that this phase of the Klan movement has been much fathered by the sales crew selling subscriptions at $10 each under the direction of Wizard Simmons and Imperial Kleagle Clarke.

The exact text of the oath of allegiance administered to new members of the Ku Klux Klan is given herewith. The asterisks are printed to take place of the Ku Klux Klan and also the officers of the order. These places are left blank in the printed oath because it is carried by Klan officials and might be lost, revealing their secret.

The oath:

You will place your left hand over your heart and raise your right hand to heaven.

SEC. I.—OBEDIENCE

(You will say) "I" —— (Pronounce your full name —— and repeat after me) "In the presence of God and Man —— most solemnly pledge, promise and [34]swear —— unconditionally —— that I will faithfully obey —— the constitution and laws —— and will willingly conform to —— all regulations, usages and requirements —— of the * * * * —— which do now exist —— or which may be hereafter enacted —— and will render at all times —— loyal respect and steadfast support —— to the Imperial Authority of same —— and will heartily heed —— all official mandates —— decrees —— edicts —— rulings and instructions —— of the I* W* thereof. —— I will yield prompt response —— to all summonses —— I having knowledge of same —— Providence alone preventing.

SEC. II.—SECRECY

"I most solemnly swear —— that I will forever —— keep sacredly secret —— the signs, words and grip —— and any and all other —— matters and knowledge —— of the * * * * —— regarding which a most rigid secrecy —— must be maintained —— which may at any time —— be communicated to me —— and will never divulge same —— nor even cause the same to be divulged —— to any person in the whole world —— unless I know positively —— that such person is a member of this Order —— in good and regular standing —— and not even then —— unless it be —— for the best interest of this Order.

"I most sacredly vow —— and most positively swear —— that I will not yield to bribe —— flattery —— threats —— passion —— punishment —— persecution —— persuasion —— nor any enticements whatever —— coming from or offered by —— any person or persons —— male or female —— for the purpose of —— obtaining from me —— a secret or secret information —— of the * * * * —— I will die rather than divulge same —— so help me God ——

AMEN!"

You will drop your hands.

GENTLEMEN (or SIR):

You will wait in patience and peace until you are [35]informed of the decision of the E* C* and his * in klonklave assembled

You will place your left hand over your heart and raise your right hand to heaven.

SEC. III.—FIDELITY

(You will say) "I" —— (pronounce your full name —— and repeat after me) "Before God —— and in the presence of —— these mysterious *smen —— on my sacred honor —— do most solemnly and sincerely pledge —— promise and swear —— that I will diligently guard and faithfully foster —— every interest of the * * * * —— and will maintain —— its social cast and dignity.

"I swear that I will not recommend —— any person for membership in this Order —— whose mind is unsound —— or whose reputation I know to be bad —— or whose character is doubtful —— or whose loyalty to our country —— is in any way questionable.

"I swear that I will pay promptly —— all just and legal demands —— made upon me to defray the expenses —— of my * and this Order —— when same are due or called for.

"I swear that I will protect the property —— of the * * * * —— of any nature whatsoever —— and if any should be intrusted to my keeping —— I will properly keep —— or rightly use same —— and will freely and promptly surrender same —— on official demand —— or if ever I am banished from —— or voluntarily discontinue —— my membership in this Order.

"I swear that I will most determinedly —— maintain peace and harmony —— in all the deliberations —— of the gatherings or assemblies —— of the I* E* —— and of any subordinate jurisdiction —— or * thereof.

"I swear that I will most strenuously —— discourage selfishness —— and selfish political ambition —— on the part of myself or any *sman.

[36]"I swear that I will never allow —— personal friendship —— blood or family relationship —— nor personal —— political —— or professional prejudice —— malice nor ill-will —— to influence me in casting my vote —— for the election or rejection —— of an applicant —— for membership in this Order —— God being my helper ——

AMEN!"

You will drop your hands.

You will place your left hand over your heart and raise your right hand to heaven.

SEC. IV.—*ISHNESS

(You will say) "I" —— (Pronounce your full name —— and repeat after me) "Most solemnly pledge, promise and swear —— that I will never slander —— defraud —— receive —— or in any manner wrong

—— the * * * * —— a *sman —— nor a *sman's family —— nor will I suffer the same to be done —— if I can prevent it.

"I swear that I will be faithful —— in defending and protecting —— the home —— reputation —— and physical and business interest —— of a *sman —— and that of a *sman's family.

"I swear that I will at any time —— without hesitating —— go to the assistance or rescue —— of a *sman in any way —— at his call I will answer —— I will be truly *ish toward *smen —— in all things honorable.

"I swear that I will not allow —— any animosity —— friction nor ill-will —— to arise and remain —— between myself and a *sman —— but will be constant in my efforts —— to promote real *ishness —— among the members of this Order.

"I swear that I will keep secure to myself —— a secret of a *sman —— when same is committed to me —— in the sacred bond of *smanship —— the crime of violating THIS solemn oath —— treason against the United States of America —— rape —— and malicious murder —— alone excepted.

"I most solemnly assert and affirm —— that to the Government of the United States of America —— and any [37]State thereof —— of which I may become a resident —— I sacredly swear —— an unqualified allegiance —— above any other and every kind of government —— in the whole world —— I here and now —— pledge my life —— my property —— my vote —— and my sacred honor —— to uphold its flag —— its Constitution —— and Constitutional laws —— and will protect —— defend —— and enforce same unto death.

"I swear that I will most zealously —— and valiantly —— shield and preserve —— by any and all —— justifiable means and methods —— the sacred constitutional rights —— and privileges of —— free public schools —— free speech —— free press —— separation of church and state —— liberty —— white supremacy —— just laws —— and the pursuit of happiness —— against any encroachment —— of any nature —— by any person or persons —— political party or parties —— religious sect or people —— native, naturalized or foreign —— of any race —— color —— creed —— lineage or tongue whatsoever.

"All to which I have sworn by THIS oath —— I will seal with my blood —— be Thou my witness —— Almighty God —— AMEN!"

You will drop your hands.

OLD PLEDGE OF LOYALTY

APPELLATION

This Organization shall be styled and denominated, The Order of the (then follows three stars; no other name given).

CREED

We, the Order of the * * *, reverentially acknowledge the majesty and supremacy of the Divine Being, and recognize the goodness and providence of the same. And we recognize our relation to the United States Government, the supremacy of the Constitution, the Constitutional Laws thereof, and the Union of States thereunder.

OBJECTS OF THE ORDER

This is an institution of Chivalry, Humanity, Mercy, and Patriotism; embodying in its genius and its principles all that is chivalric in conduct, noble in sentiment, generous in manhood, and patriotic in purpose; its peculiar object being,

First: To protect the weak, the innocent, and the defenseless, from the indignities, wrongs, and outrages, of the lawless, the violent, and the brutal; to relieve the injured and oppressed; to succor the suffering and unfortunate, and especially the widows and orphans of Confederate soldiers.

Second: To protect and defend the Constitution of the United States, and all laws passed in conformity thereto, and to protect the States and the people thereof from all invasion from any source whatever.

Third: To aid and assist in the execution of all constitutional laws, and to protect the people from unlawful seizure, and from trial except by their peers in conformity to the laws of the land.

Note the vast difference between this and the following page. One, the pledge to all that is right and uplifting—the other to a single autocrat. The above was formed for the protection and enforcement of law—the Kleagle's pledge, merely a vow to do anything that the Imperial Wizard Simmons might see fit.

MODERN KLEAGLE'S PLEDGE OF LOYALTY

I, the undersigned, in order to be a regular appointed KlEagle of the Invisible Empire, Knights of the Ku Klux Klan (Incorporated), do freely and voluntarily promise, pledge and fully guarantee a lofty respect, whole-hearted loyalty and an unwavering devotion at all times and under any and all circumstances and conditions from this day and date forward to William Joseph Simmons as Imperial Wizard and Emperor of the Invisible Empire, Knights of the Ku Klux Klan (Incorporated). I shall work in all respects in perfect harmony with him and under his authority and directions, in all his plans for the extension and government of the Society, and under his directions, with any and all of my officially superior officers duly appointed by him.

I shall at any and all times be faithful and true in all things, and most especially in preventing and suppressing any factions, cisms or conspiracies against him or his plans and purposes or the peace and harmony of the Society which may arise or attempt to arise. I shall discourage and strenuously oppose any degree of disloyalty or disrespect on the part of myself or any klansman, any where and at any time or place, towards him as the founder and as the supreme chief governing head of the Society above named.

This pledge, promise and guarantee I make is a condition precedent to my appointment stated above, and the continuity of my appointment as a KlEagle, and it is fully agreed that any deviation by me from this pledge will instantly automatically cancel and completely void my appointment together with all its prerogatives, my membership in the Society, and I shall forfeit all remunerations which may be then due me.

I make this solemn pledge on my Oath of Allegiance and on my integrity and honor as a man and as a klansman, with serious purpose to keep same inviolate.

    Done in the city of ...., State of
    .... on this the ....
    day of .... A.D. 19...
    Signed ....
    Address ....
    Witness: ....
    Address ....

This is the oath taken by Kleagles in the Ku Klux Klan. It binds the Kleagle to "Imperial Wizard" Simmons personally in an almost slavish fashion. The oath is taken as a pledge of loyalty to Simmons and not to the order.

CHAPTER VI

HOW THE DOLLARS ROLL IN

The Klan Claims to Have 500,000 to 700,000 Members. Plan to get College Boys.

The Ku Klux Klan claims to have 500,000 to 700,000 members. As a matter of fact it is generally believed that that number is a hot air figure. It offers a basis for some interesting figures on the money that has changed hands, however.

Every person initiated must pay $10 as an initiation fee. Kleagles who have left the order say that the "initiation" fee is called a "donation" so that the Klan can escape paying income tax to the government, because dues in clubs and societies are taxable.

Of the $10, the kleagle who enrolls the member gets $4. The king kleagle, or state salesmanager, gets $1. The cyclops, or division manager, gets 50 cents. Clarke, the Imperial Kleagle, gets $3 and the office of Imperial Wizard Simmons gets $1.50. On this basis of 700,000 members, Clarke has collected more than $2,000,000. So far as known no public accounting ever has been made.

In addition the person initiated pays $6.50 for a mask, or helmet, and a robe. This he must purchase from the Gate City Manufacturing Company of Atlanta, owned by Clarke. Clarke's fortune grows every time a new member is taken in. If the Klansman rides a horse in ceremonies he must buy a robe for $14—also from Clarke's company.

WATER AT $10 A QUART

Another source of revenue to Clarke is the water used in initiations. It comes from the Chattahoochee river (Indian for "muddy water") near Atlanta. It is sent [41]around the country as special Ku Klux Klan liquid without which an initiation cannot be held. It costs $10 a quart, money to be paid to Clarke.

Simmons and Clarke live in costly houses on Peachtree road, outside of Atlanta. It is explained that their homes were presented to them by the Klan. It also is explained that some of the money of the Klan goes to Lanier university, near Atlanta, where young students are to be trained to spread the Ku Klux Klan to every village of the country.

AFTER THE COLLEGE BOYS

In addition to the general membership, Simmons started a plan to get college boys into the Ku Klux Klan at $1 a head and with a charge of $5 for masks and regalia. The watchword for the college boys was to be "Kuno." Simmons, according to kleagles who deserted him, explained that he got the college idea from the German militarism system, which started to train boys for the army when they were in school. Simmons wrote this inspiration to attract college boys:

"Klannishners is your creed and faith; therefore, let no angel, man or devil break you from its glorious anchorage. Then when the end of your initiation shall have been reached in this life and you have been summoned to take your place as an inhabitant of the Invisible Empire, as you pass through the veil you can say to the world in tones of truth triumphant: "I have kept the Faith!" Thus preserving your honor by a faithful allegiance your life shall not have been lived in vain."

THE BOOK OF "KLORAN"

The ceremony of initiation is contained in a copyrighted book called the Kloran written by Imperial Wizard Simmons. The Bible is opened at the 12th Chapter of Romans.

These songs are sung:

[42]
We meet in cordial greetings In this our sacred cave To pledge anew our compact With hearts sincere and brave; A band of faithful Klansmen Knights of the K.K.K. We all will stand together Forever and for aye.
Chorus: Home, home, country and home; Klansmen, we'll live and die For our country and home.
Her honor, love and justice Must actuate us all, Before our sturdy phalanx All hate and strife shall fall. In union we'll labor Wherever we may roam, To shield a Klansman's welfare, His country, name and home.

KLEXOLOGY

(Tune—America)

"God of Eternity, Guide, guard our great country, Our homes and store. Keep our great state to Thee; Its people right and free In us Thy glory be Forevermore."

CHAPTER VII

KU KLUX KLAN AND THE JEWS

"Drive them out of the United States" are the words that are used to enlist Jew-haters into the ranks.

In spite of the fact that ever since the beginning of the American colonies, in the war of the revolution and in other national crises, great Jews have helped to make the United States what it is today, the Ku Klux Klan recruits misguided members on the representation that it has found a scheme to drive the Jews out of the country. Anti-Jewish propaganda is used particularly in large cities and in smaller communities where racial and religious flames may be fanned in order to win members and money for the Ku Klux.

The Searchlight, the official paper of the Klan, teems with anti-Jewish literature. Secret documents and stories are passed around privately among the organizers and used in gaining recruits.

"Chaplain" Ridley is one of the most rabid of the campaigners against the Jews. He never lets an opportunity go by to ridicule Jews and stir up prejudice.

In the first place, Jews are barred from the Ku Klux Klan. In a questionnaire that must be filled in by those who are initiated these questions are asked:

"Are you a gentile or a jew? What is your religious faith? Of what church are you a member (if any)? Of what religious faith are your parents?"

CHAPLAIN ATTACKS JEWS

"Chaplain" Ridley in *The Searchlight*, writes:

"I cannot help being what I am racially. I am not a Jew, [44]nor a negro nor a foreigner. I am an Anglo-Saxon white man, so ordained by the hand and will of God, and so constituted and trained that I cannot conscientiously take either my politics or my religion from some secluded ass on the other side of the world.

"Now, if somebody else happens to be a Jew, I can't help it any more than he can. Or if he happens to be black, I can't help that, either. If he were born under a foreign flag, I couldn't help it—but there is one thing I can do. I can object to his un-American propaganda being preached in my home or practiced in the solemn assembly of real Americans."

The Searchlight constantly mixes Jews and negroes in ridiculous "movements." For instance, one writer in the issue of July 30, 1921, declares that his investigations have demonstrated that Jewish plotters are stirring up the negroes to make a race war so that the government will be destroyed.

The writer goes on:

"For the same reason, the Jew is interested in overthrowing Christian Russia. But remember, he does not intend to stop at Russia. Through his Third Internationale of Moscow he is working to overthrow all the Gentile Governments of the world. I am enclosing an editorial clipped from The New York *World* of Saturday, July 23. You will keep in mind that *The World* is Jew-owned, as is every other newspaper in New York City except the Tribune. * * * In all my twenty-five years traveling about over this continent I have never met a disloyal American who failed to be either foreign-born or a Semite. With the best wishes for the success of the Ku Klux Klan."

HOW TO THROW JEWS OUT

In the instructions to kleagles, who sell memberships in the Klan, the anti-Jewish feeling in some communities is appealed to in this manner:

"The Jew patronizes only the Jew unless it is impossible to do so. Therefore, we klansmen, the only real Americans, must, by the same methods, protect ourselves, and practice by actual application the teachings of klannishness. With this policy faithfully adhered to, it will not be long before the Jew will be forced out of business by our practice of his own business methods, for when the time comes when klansmen trade only with klansmen then the days of the Jews' success in business will be numbered and the Invisible Empire can drive them from the shores of our own America."

Another favorite way to create interest in the anti-Jewish movement is to represent that Imperial Kleagle Clarke has in hand the organization of a nation-wide Jewish society to oppose the Sons of Israel. This society is to be created by Jews who are in the pay of Kleagle Clarke and who are really traitors to their own co-religionists. Spies working in the ranks of the Sons of Israel will keep the Ku Klux Klan informed of what the Sons of Israel are doing and finally a clash between the two organizations is to be engineered, to the destruction of both. Of course this is the wildest sort of propaganda, but it demonstrates how the agents play with fire in order to get members.

"SEARCHLIGHT" AND THE JEWS

Among the articles in *The Searchlight* there are those headed, "A Message from Jerusalem—Esau the Wanderer must Pay for His Pottage—the Mightiest Weapons for the Jews are Pounds and Pence."

"Doesn't Think Much of the Jews."

"Jewish Rabbi Gets Rabid."

A paragraph from "Doesn't Think Much of the Jews," published Feb. 12, 1921, contains this passage:

"Their religion is to control wealth and thereby control all nations. And you cannot deny but they are doing so under false names. Jews are entering into every Government, every nation on earth except China and Japan, where their heavenly God received little recognition. They spread their ingenious religion that strangled the ignorant and credulous by causing dissension to their advantage."

CHAPTER VIII

KU KLUX KLAN AND THE CATHOLICS

Misrepresentation of Oath of Knights of Columbus is Used to excite Religious Hatred in order to get money.

Just as the organizers of the Ku Klux Klan misrepresent the Jews in order to get members and money for their order, they go to great lengths to create prejudice against Catholics. In some communities anti-Catholic arguments are thought to be those that will bring the most members into the fold. Fake documents and false statements on printed cards that can be slyly passed from hand to hand are used for this purpose. Anti-Catholic lies that can be hurled at Klansmen at meetings to inspire them to get in more members and increase the incomes of the "imperial wizard," the kleagles and other officers are spread around.

One of these documents is a card entitled "Do You Know?" A kleagle of the Klan asked the King Kleagle of his state for some literature that he could employ to stir up interest in the Klan. In a short time the kleagle received the literature from the Gate City Manufacturing Company of Atlanta, Ga., a company promoted by "Imperial Kleagle" Clarke. The supply of literature contained 100 copies of a card bearing the heading "Do You Know?"

Another document that is sent broadcast to foment religious unrest and hatred is a fake oath ascribed to the Knights of Columbus, which is composed of Catholics and which has published the oath that its members take. Before reading the fake oath, it will be well to examine the real oath.

REAL K. OF C. OATH

The bona fide oath that is taken by men initiated into the Knights of Columbus, and which, it has been proven, is the correct oath follows:

"I swear to support the Constitution of the United States. I pledge myself, as a Catholic citizen and Knight of Columbus, to enlighten myself fully upon my duties as a citizen and to conscientiously perform such duties entirely in the interest of my country and regardless of all personal consequences. I pledge myself to do all in my power to preserve the integrity and purity of the ballot, and to promote reverence and respect for law and order. I promise to practice my religion openly and consistently, but without ostentation, and to so conduct myself in public affairs, and in the exercise of public virtue as to reflect nothing but credit upon our Holy Church, to the end that she may flourish and our country prosper to the greater honor and glory of God."

BOGUS K. OF C. OATH

We can now appreciate the animus behind the bogus oath that is ascribed to the Knights of Columbus by the Ku Klux Klan. This fraudulent oath, as used by the recruiting organization of kleagles of Ku Klux follows:

"I, ——— ———, now in the presence of Almighty God, the blessed Virgin Mary, the blessed St. John the Baptist, the Holy Apostles, St. Peter and St. Paul, and all the saints, sacred host of Heaven, and to you, my Ghostly Father, the Superior General of the Society of Jesus, founded by St. Ignatius Loyola, in the pontification of Paul the III, and continued to the present, do by the womb of the Virgin, the matrix of God, and the rod of Jesus Christ, declare and swear that His Holiness the Pope is Christ's vicegerent and is the true and only head of the Catholic or Universal Church throughout the earth; and that by virtue of the keys of binding and loosing given His Holiness by [48]my Saviour, Jesus Christ, he hath power to depose heretical Kings, Princes, states, Commonwealths and Governments and they may be safely destroyed. Therefore to the utmost of my power I will defend this doctrine and His Holiness's right and custom against all usurpers of the heretical or Protestant authority whatever, especially the Lutheran Church of Germany, Holland, Denmark, Sweden and Norway, and the now pretended authority and Churches of England and Scotland, and the branches of same now established in Ireland and on the Continent of America and elsewhere, and all adherents in regard that they may be usurped and heretical opposing the sacred Mother Church of Rome.

"I do now denounce and disown any allegiance as due to any heretical King, Prince, or state, named Protestant or liberals, or obedience to any of their laws, Magistrates, or officers.

"I do further declare that the doctrine of the Churches of England and Scotland, of the Calvinists, Huguenots and others of the name of Protestants or Masons to be damnable, and they themselves to be damned who will not forsake the same.

"I do further declare that I will help, assist and advise all or any of His Holiness' agents, in any place where I should be, in Switzerland, Holland, Ireland or America, or in any other kingdom or territory I shall come to, and do my utmost to extirpate the heretical Protestant or Masonic doctrines and to destroy all their pretended powers, legal or otherwise.

MORE OF IT

"I do further promise and declare that, notwithstanding that I am dispensed with to assume any religion heretical for the propaganda of the Mother Church's interest, to keep secret and private all her agents' counsels from time to time, as they instruct me, and not divulge, directly or indirectly, by word, writing or circumstances whatever, [49]but to execute all that should be proposed, given in charge or discovered unto me by you, my Ghostly Father, or any of this sacred order.

"I do further promise and declare that I will have no opinion or will of my own or any mental reservation whatsoever, even as a corpse or cadaver (perinde ac cadaver), but will unhesitatingly obey each and every command that I may receive from my superiors in the militia of the Pope and of Jesus Christ.

"That I will go to any part of the world whithersoever I may be sent, to the frozen regions north, jungles of India, to the centers of civilization of Europe or to the wild haunts of the barbarous savages of America without murmuring or repining, and will be submissive in all things whatsoever is communicated to me.

AND STILL MORE

"I do further promise and declare that I will, when opportunity presents, make and wage relentless war, secretly and openly, against all heretics, Protestants and Masons, as I am directed to do, to extirpate them from the face of the whole earth; and that I will spare neither age, sex or condition, and that I will hang, burn, waste, boil, flay, strangle, and bury alive these infamous heretics; rip up the stomachs and wombs of their women and crash their infants' heads against the walls in order to annihilate their execrable race. That when the same cannot be done openly, I will secretly use the poisonous cup, strangulation cord, the steel of the poniard or the leaden bullet, regardless of the honor, rank, dignity or authority of the persons, whatever may be their condition in life, either public or private, as I at any time may be directed so to do by any agents of the Pope or superior of the Brotherhood of the Holy Father of the Society of Jesus.

"In confirmation of which I hereby dedicate my life, soul and all corporate powers, and with the dagger which I now receive I will subscribe my name written in my blood in [50]testimony thereof; and should I prove false or weaken in my determination, may my brethren and fellow soldiers of the militia of the Pope cut off my hands and feet and my throat from ear to ear, my belly opened and sulphur burned therein with all the punishment that can be inflicted upon me on earth and my soul shall be tortured by demons in eternal hell forever.

NEARING THE END NOW

"That I will in voting always vote for a K. of C. in preference to a Protestant, especially a Mason, and that I will leave my party so to do; that if two Catholics are on the ticket I will satisfy myself which is the better supporter of Mother Church and vote accordingly.

"That I will not deal with or employ a Protestant if in my power to deal with or employ a Catholic. That I will place Catholic girls in Protestant families, that a weekly report may be made of the inner movements of the heretics.

"That I will provide myself with arms and ammunition that I may be in readiness when the word is passed or I am commanded to defend the church, either as an individual or with the militia of the Pope.

"All of which I, —— ——, do swear by the blessed Trinity and blessed sacrament which I am now to receive to perform and on my part to keep this, my oath.

"In testimony whereof, I take this most holy and blessed sacrament of the Eucharist and witness the same further with my name written with the point of this dagger dipped in my own blood and seal it in the face of this holy sacrament." (Excerpts from "Contested election case of Eugene C. Bonniwell against Thomas S. Butler," as appears in the Congressional Record —— House, Feb. 15, 1913, at pages 3215, &c., and ordered printed therein "by unanimous consent." Attached thereto and printed (on page 3216) as a part of said report as above.)

The above spurious oath, and others like it, have been found to be fraudulent, both by the courts and by an [51]investigation made by Masonic bodies. The above oath made its appearance according to a book published by Maurice Francis Egan, for eleven years United States Minister to Denmark, and John B. Kennedy, in 1912. Messrs. Egan and Kennedy explain it as follows:

"It was filed by Mr. Eugene C. Bonniwell of Pennsylvania in his charge against Thomas S. Butler before the Committee of Elections No. 1, in Congress, when Mr. Bonniwell stated that it had been used against him as a Fourth Degree Knight of Columbus in an election contest. Mr. Butler, in his defense, stated that he had refrained from condemning the 'oath,' until election day, although he did not believe it to be genuine, because he feared to give it notoriety.

"Far from being disconcerted by the airing of this delectable document in Congress, those profiting by its circulation seized upon its inclusion in the Congressional Record to give it an air of authority by printing on future copies the annotation 'Copied from the Congressional Record, &c.,' not pausing, however, to explain the circumstances under which it was allowed to appear in that official journal."

EDITORS ARE CONVICTED

A.M. Morrison and Garfield E. Morrison, editors of the *Morning Journal* of Mankato, Minn., charged E.M. Lawless, editor of the Waterville, Minn., *Sentinel* with having taken the bogus oath. Lawless took the case to court and the two Morrisons were convicted. The foreman of the jury was a Methodist minister.

In 1914 the bogus oath came to light in California. The Knights of Columbus asked a committee of two, 32nd and 33rd degree, Masons, Past or Past Grand Masters of Masonry of that state, to make an investigation of all the rituals, pledges and oaths used by the Knights of Columbus. The Masonic committee gave out a report saying that they had made such an investigation. They found that the [52]ceremonies of the Knights of Columbus were embodied in four degrees "intended to teach and inculcate principles that lie at the foundations of every great religion and every great state."

WHAT MASONS REPORTED

Their report continued:

"Our examination was made primarily to ascertain whether or not a certain alleged oath * * * which has been printed and widely circulated was in fact used by the Order and whether * * * any oath, obligation or pledge was used which was or would be offensive to Protestants or Masons. * * * We find that neither the alleged oath nor any such oath or pledge bearing the remotest resemblance thereto in matter, manner, spirit or purpose is used or forms a part of the ceremonies of any degree of the Knights of Columbus. The alleged oath is scurrilous, wicked and libelous and must be the invention of an impious and venomous mind. * * * There is no propaganda proposed or taught against Protestants or Masons or persons not of Catholic faith. * * * We can find nothing in the entire ceremonials of the Order that to our minds could be objected to by any person."

The Searchlight, official organ of the Ku Klux, contains many articles that misrepresent the Catholics. For instance, of Feb. 26, 1921, *The Searchlight* had an article which was captioned: "Facts Gathered by the Knights of Luther from the Washington Bureau of Statistics":

CHARGES OF "KNIGHTS OF LUTHER"

Without one word to support them, the following were printed as "facts":

"The National Democratic Committee is by majority a Roman Catholic body. It usually has a Roman Catholic President and secretary.

[53]"Catholics influenced the national campaign which elected Wilson.

"The President's private secretary is a Roman Catholic.

"Over 70 per cent. of all appointments made by President Wilson are Catholics. Their influence is so powerful it compels the homage of those in authority.

"Five States now have Catholic Administrations.

"Thirty-one States have Roman Catholic Democratic Central Committees.

"Twenty thousand public schools have one-half Catholic teachers.

"Over 100,000 public schools now contribute a part or all of the school tax to Catholic Churches and schools.

"Six hundred public schools use Catholic readers and teach from them the Roman Catholic catechism.

"Sixty-two per cent. of all offices of the United States, both elective and appointive, are now held by Roman Catholics.

"New York, Chicago, Baltimore, Philadelphia, Buffalo, Cleveland, Toledo, St. Louis, Los Angeles, San Francisco and Boston now have 75 per cent. Catholic teachers in their public schools.

"In all the cities and towns of the United States of 10,000 or more inhabitants an average of over 90 per cent. of the police force are Roman Catholics.

"Roman Catholics are in the majority of the City Council of 10,000 cities and towns of the United States."

MORE OF THE SAME STUFF

The Searchlight continues:

"We will now look at the results of Catholic teaching on vice and virtue. The history of assassins of heads of Governments in the past is a history of murderous Roman Catholics. In 90 per cent. of the cases where criminals are executed for crimes committed, the victims of the execution have a priest at their elbow to administer the last sacrament.

[54]"The man who shot Roosevelt was a Roman Catholic.

"The man who shot President Garfield was a Roman Catholic.

"The man who shot President Lincoln was a Roman Catholic.

"The plot that took the life of Lincoln emanated from Roman Catholic influence in the house of a Roman Catholic.

"Abraham Lincoln said, 'I do not pretend to be a prophet but, though not a prophet, I see a very dark cloud on our horizon, and that cloud is coming from Rome. It is filled with tears and blood. The true motive power is secreted behind the walls of the Vatican, the colleges and schools of the Jesuits, the convents of the nuns, and the confessional boxes of Rome,' and such opinions cost the Nation his life.

"Over 65 per cent. of prison convicts of all grades and of all kinds of prisoners are Roman Catholics, while less than 5 per cent. are graduates of our public schools.

"These statements are astounding when we remember that only about 12-½ per cent. of the entire population of the United States are Roman Catholics, while the other 87-½ per cent. are not."

CHAPTER IX

KU KLUX KLAN AND THE MASONS

Iowa and Missouri Jurisdiction Grand Masters Issue Public Denunciations Against the Klan.

Promoters of the Ku Klux Klan brag that most of its members are Masons. Whether this is true no one on the outside can tell. It is known, however, that the kleagles or salesmen, who solicit members in a community try to play upon the Masonic spirit to help along their game. That this is done with the disapproval of the leading Masonic bodies of the country is shown by the action of the grand commanders of the Iowa and Missouri jurisdictions. They have issued public denunciations of the operations and purposes of the Klan, especially that feature that resorts to the masking of members when they are taking part in Klan rites. The examples of Iowa and Missouri are being followed by Masons in other states.

IOWA GRAND MASTER'S STATEMENT

Amos N. Alberson of Washington, Iowa, grand master of that state, has directed a communication to all Masonic lodges under his jurisdiction as follows:

"Whereas, It has become known to your grand master that a certain 'Ku Klux Klan' has been and is now organizing within this jurisdiction an alleged 'secret and invisible empire'; and,

"Whereas, It is reported that its organizers and agents have stated and intimated to members of our craft that the said 'Ku Klux Klan' is in effect an adjunct of Freemasonry and in accord with its principles and purposes; and,

[56]"Whereas, Any such statement or intimation is absolutely false and untrue, in that Masonry can not and does not approve of or ally itself with any organization or movement, secret or public, that proposes to subvert or supersede the processes of orderly representative government 'of the people, for the people, and by the people'; nor one that appeals to bigotry and endeavors to foster hatred of any nationality, class, religious faith or sect, as such.

THE SOLEMN CHARGE

"Therefore, I, Amos N. Alberson, grand master of Masons in Iowa, do solemnly charge each and all of the regular Masons in Iowa, now as heretofore when you were made a Mason, that 'in the state you are to be a quiet and peaceable subject, true to your government and just to your country; you are not to countenance disloyalty or rebellion, but patiently submit to legal authority, and conform with cheerfulness to the government of the country in which you live.'

\CITES MASONIC OBLIGATION

"Furthermore, I charge each and all, that as our fathers have framed the truly Masonic principles of liberty and conscience, equality before the law, and fraternity among men into the constitutions of this nation and state, we as Free Masons and citizens of this republic are obligated to perform our full moral and civic duty, to promote and enforce an orderly administration of justice and equity, acting openly that it may be known of all men."

Grand Master Alberson further orders and directs "that this letter to the craft be read aloud at the next meeting, whether regular or special, of each lodge throughout this jurisdiction; that it shall be made of record, and due notice of the same circulated among the brethrens, that it may come to the knowledge of all Masons in Iowa."

MISSOURI'S ACTION ON KLAN

William F. Johnson, grand master of the Carterlin Grand Lodge of Missouri Ancient-Free and Accepted Masons made this statement at the annual meeting of the grand lodge, which indorsed it:

"As the impression seems to prevail in some sections, that the Masonic fraternity is directly or indirectly associated with or furthering this secret organization (Ku Klux Klan), and as I have been asked on numerous occasions what relations, if any, our fraternity bears to such secret society or order, it is well that the seal of disapproval be positively placed by this grand lodge upon this secret organization, which assumes to itself the right and authority to administer law and punish crimes.

"Nothing is more destructive of free government than secret control. The arraying of race against race, color against color, sect against sect is destructive of peace and harmony, which is the great end we, as Free Masons, have in view. We profess and boast that we are true to our government and just to our country.

IS SUBVERSIVE OF THE REPUBLIC

"We can not, as Free Masons and good citizens, recognize the right of any secret society or combination of men to assume unto themselves the right to administer law and to inflict punishment upon their fellow men. Such an assumption is subversive of our republican institutions, contrary to the great principles of Free Masonry.

"An organization that practices censorship of private conduct behind the midnight anonymity of mask and robe, and enforces its secret decrees with the weapons of whips and tar and feathers must ultimately merit and receive the condemnation of those who believe in courts, open justice and good citizenship."

CHAPTER X

KU KLUX KLAN AND THE NEGRO

Members of the Klan take an oath to Bring about White Supremacy, notwithstanding the Constitution, which guarantees the Negro Equal Rights.

Under the constitution of the United States, the negro is guaranteed equal rights with all other citizens. When the President of the United States is sworn into office he takes an oath to uphold the constitution and the laws passed under it. Every senator, congressman, governor and other important officer in the United States and in each of the states is sworn to uphold the constitution.

But the members of the Ku Klux Klan take an oath that puts the constitution at naught. They swear to bring about "white supremacy." Taken in conjunction with the speeches and writings of their leaders, this oath shows that the Klansmen intend to work together to create strife against the negro, to belittle him and his family, his churches, his business, his social societies and other things that are dear to him. The Klan is determined to put the negro out of business in the United States and to drive him back to Africa.

As is all other main objects—the warfare on Jews, Catholics and foreign born—the Klan intends to follow its own laws in dealing with the negro. The writings of its leaders are very plain on that point.

In his oath the Klansman swears:

"I swear that I will most zealously and valiantly shield and preserve by any and all justifiable means and methods White Supremacy——

"All to which I have sworn by this oath. I will seal with my blood by Thou my witness, Almighty God. Amen."

[59]Prominent lawyers who have examined this oath declare that it really is an oath upholding mob rule and that any time the Klansman is given orders he will follow his leaders in a crusade outside the constitution of the United States that might lead to serious trouble and bloodshed.

Chaplain Ridley of the Ku Klux Klan has written in *The Searchlight* on white supremacy as follows:

"Back in the days of the reconstruction the fathers gathered at the call of the low, shrill whistle and rode into immortal fame, rescuing a threatened civilization and making real once more the White Man's Supremacy. Klansmen of to-day, whether they assemble in the mountains of Maine, or 'neath the shadows of the great Rockies, or on the plains of the Wonderful West, or amid the trailing vines and wild flowers of Dixie, meet to keep alive the memory of these men and preserve the traditions of those days when the souls of men were tried as if by fire."

In Texas a white man who testified in behalf of an accused negro—he merely told the truth under oath as he knew it—was tarred and feathered by masked men.

The Searchlight has printed column after column of anti-negro stuff, mostly under anonymous names or under the titles of organizations whose addresses are not given. One such resolution adopted by the

"Patriotic Societies of Atlanta" condemns Rev. Ashby Jones, a minister, for inviting an honorable negro to an interracial meeting and for addressing the negro as "mister."

Here are some of the titles of articles in *The Searchlight*, showing its evident purpose of stirring up racial feelings:

"Social Equality Put Under Ban."

"Negroes Must Serve on Chain Gangs Now."

"Separate Cars for Negroes."

"White Woman Marries a Negro."

The Searchlight condemned President Harding for appointing Henry Lincoln Johnson, a negro, as register of deeds.

CHAPTER XI

THE KU KLUX KLAN AND WOMEN

Here is the proclamation issued by Imperial Wizard Simmons, making Mrs. Elizabeth Tyler his "grand chief of staff" to have charge of the women's organization to be affiliated with the Ku Klux Klan:

"To all Genii, Grand Dragons and Hydras of Realms, Grand Goblins and Kleagles of Domains, Grand Titans and Furies of Provinces, Giants, Exalted Cyclops and Terrors of Cantons, and to all citizens of the Invisible Empire, Knights of the Ku Klux Klan, in the name of our valiant and venerated dead, I affectionately greet you:

"In view of our Nation's need and as an additional force in helping on the great work of conserving, protecting and making effective the great principles of our Anglo-Saxon civilization and American ideals and institutions, the Imperial Kloncilium, in regular session assembled, after deliberate care and earnest prayer, decided that there shall be established within the bounds and under the supreme authority and government of the Invisible Empire an organization that will admit the splendid women of our great national commonwealth, who are now citizens with us in directing the affairs of the Nation. Which decision of the Imperial Kloncilium I have officially ratified after serious, careful and devoted consideration of all matters and things involved by this move.

"In view of the foregoing, I hereby officially declare and proclaim that such organization does now exist in prospect. Plans, methods, ritualism and regulations of same are now in process of formation and will be perfected at an early date and officially announced.

"I do farther proclaim that in order to have the proper assistance in the formation and perfecting of this [61]organization, I have this day and date selected and officially appointed Mary Elizabeth Tyler of Atlanta, Fulton county, Ga., to be my grand chief of staff, to have immediate charge of work pertaining to said woman's organization under my authority and direction.

"Further information will be duly and officially communicated from time to time.

"Done in the Aulic of His Majesty, Imperial Wizard, Emperor of the Invisible Empire, Knights of the Ku Klux Klan, in the Imperial City of Atlanta, Commonwealth of Georgia, United States of America, on this, the ninth day of the ninth month of the year of our Lord, 1921.

"Duly signed and sealed by His Majesty,

William Joseph Simmons,
"Imperial Wizard."

CHAPTER XII

ATROCITIES COMMITTED IN THE NAME OF KU KLUX KLAN

Ku Klux Klan Knights of Beaumont, Texas, issue a justification for taking the law into Their own hands.

Confession that the Ku Klux Klan uses tar and feathers and the lash to punish persons whose actions it condemns is made by the Klansmen of Beaumont, Tex. The Beaumont Ku Klux Klan organization tarred and feathered Dr. J.S. Paul and R.F. Scott and later acknowledged, under its official seal, that its members did the job.

"Knights of the Ku Klux Klan, No. 7, Beaumont, Texas," admitted taking the law into their own hands in a statement dated July 21, 1921. This statement was made to the editors of two newspapers of Beaumont. It sought to justify the "tar and feather party" and gave warning that the "heavy hand of the Ku Klux Klan" was waiting to yank other persons from their beds in case they came into its displeasure.

SHOW SIMMONS MISREPRESENTS

Grand Wizard William J. Simmons has declared publicly that the Ku Klux did not indulge in midnight raids on defenseless victims whom it tarred and feathered. He has defended the Ku Klux Klan by ascribing these unlawful actions to imposters who use the regalia of the Ku Klux. The Beaumont incident proves that the Ku Klux not only was responsible for assaults on Dr. Paul and Scott, but that it boasted of its exploits with them.

LETTER ADMITS USE OF TAR

The Paul-Scott "party" occurred on May 8. Its details were telegraphed all over the country. The letter to the two Beaumont newspapers the following July read:

"Your publication since the organization of the Ku Klux Klan in the city of Beaumont has on various occasions published information concerning and pertaining to the affairs of this organization. We believe, as you do, that a newspaper should serve the best interests of its constituency and that all legitimate news should be given the public through its columns. During the past two months items have appeared in your paper relative to the case of the Ku Klux Klan and its connection with Dr. J.S. Paul.

"Now, that you and the public may be fully informed of the true facts in the case, the Klan has assembled and herewith hands you an intelligent, true and correct history of the entire matter. The Klan suggests that this summary of facts be published in the columns of your paper not later than Sunday, July 24, 1921, and that it be published verbatim, according to the enclosed copy, typographical errors excepted.

Knights of the Ku Klux Klan."

PHYSICIAN IS ACCUSED

The "intelligent, true and correct history of the entire matter" was a lengthy statement. It accused Dr. Paul of being a physician who for years had sold whisky and narcotic drugs and had performed illegal operations on women. Because he had political and financial backing grand jury proceedings against him had been squelched.

About the middle of December, 1920, R.F. Scott, who lived in Deweyville, Texas (Scott was a former member of the United States Marine corps), consulted Dr. Paul and arranged for an illegal operation. The statement declares the girl became seriously ill as a result of malpractice on [64]Dr. Paul's part and was taken from her residence to a hospital, where a serious operation was performed.

After this occurrence the girl demanded that Dr. Paul assist her in defraying the extra expense due to his negligence, and he offered her $500 to leave Beaumont. This bargain he broke and is accused of having threatened to cause her arrest for attempted blackmail, or with death if she exposed him.

MORAL LAW ABOVE WRITTEN

Her predicament was reported to the Klan and the statement says her cry was heard by men who respect the "great moral law more than the technicalities of the legal code."

The statement goes on:

"The eyes of the unknown had seen and had observed the wrong to be redressed. Dr. Paul was wealthy. His victim was a poor girl. Between the two stood the majesty of the law, draped in technicalities of changes of venue, mistrials, appeals, postponements, eminent counsel skilled in the esoteric art of protecting crime and interpreting laws involved in a mass of legal verbiage, the winding and unwinding of red tape, instead of the sinewy arm of justice, wielding the unerring sword. The law of the Klan is JUSTICE.

"Dr. Paul was approached in his office by three men on the night of May 7 and instructed to go with them. He was placed in a waiting automobile and escorted a few miles out of town. The judgment of the Klan was read to him and charges were related to him, none of which he would deny.

"LASHED, TARRED AND FEATHERED"

"In a cowardly, whimpering plea, he pleaded that others were as guilty as he. The lash was laid on his back and [65]the tar and feathers applied to his body. He was then informed of the will of the Klan that he should leave the city within forty-eight hours. Upon the return of the party to Beaumont, Dr. Paul was discharged from an automobile at the intersection of two of the main streets of the city, that he might be a warning to all of his ilk that decent men and women no longer wanted him in the community.

"Dr. Paul complied with the instructions of the Klan that he leave the city and returned for a few days to his former home at Lufkin. During this time he was constantly under the surveillance of the Klan. Within a few days he had surrounded himself with relatives and hired hench-men of his own tribe and character and returned to Beaumont.

SCOTT ALSO TARRED AND FEATHERED

"Scott, who had been constantly watched by the Klan, whose number is legion and whose eye is all-seeing and whose methods of gathering information are not known to the alien world, was apprehended and punished in the same manner Dr. Paul had been dealt with. He was taken to the woods and guarded until nightfall. His captors during this time treated him with kindness and consideration. They provided him with food and fruit to eat and ice water to drink. During the day he was questioned and admitted all the charges the Klan had accused him of. The judgment of the Klan was that he was to be given ten lashes across the bare back and that he was to be tarred and feathered.

EYES OF "UNKNOWN" ON HIM

"Scott left Beaumont on Monday, July 18, and spent the major portion of the day in Orange parading the streets and proclaimed the diabolical lie that he had been subjected to the tortures of the inquisition. He posed to the gullible [66]public and sensational newspapers as a patriot and a hero. All these things the eyes of the unknown have seen and their ears have heard. We can not be deceived and JUSTICE will no longer be mocked."

The seal of the Beaumont Klan was attached to the end of the statement.

Rev. Caleb Ridley, known as the imperial chaplain of the order, acknowledged that the Klan's purpose was to set itself up as prosecutor, jury, judge and sheriff.

PASTOR GIVES WARNING

On Aug. 26, 1921, he issued to the citizens of Dallas county, Texas, the following warning:

"To the Citizens of Dallas County, Greetings: This organization has caused to be posted the following proclamation:

"Be it known and hereby proclaimed

"That this organization is composed of native-born Americans and none other.

"That its purpose is to uphold the dignity and the authority of the law. * * *

"That this organization * * * recognizes * * * that situations frequently arise where no existing law offers a remedy.

"That this organization does * * * not countenance and will not stand for social parasites remaining in this city. It is equally opposed to the gambler, the trickster, the moral degenerate and the man who lives by his wits and is without visible means of support.

"The eye of the unknown hath seen and doth constantly observe all, white or black, who disregard this warning. 'Whatsoever thou sowest that shall you also reap.' Regardless of official, social or financial position, this warning applies to all living within the jurisdiction of this Klan.

"This warning will not be repeated.

"'Mene, Mene, Tekel, Upharsin.'

"Hereafter all communications from us will bear the official seal of the Klan.

"KNIGHTS OF THE KU KLUX KLAN."

KU KLUX KLAN SHOOTS SHERIFF

The attitude of members of the Ku Klux Klan toward officers of the law was demonstrated on October 1, 1921, in Lorena, Tex., when the Ku Klux Klan shot Sheriff Bob Buchanan of McLennan county, when he attempted to stop a parade of Masked Knights.

Without getting an official permit to hold the parade, the Ku Klux Klan announced that it would be held at 8:30 p.m. The sheriff notified the community that the parade was against the law and that he would not allow it. The word was carried to the Ku Klux Klan leaders. Messages were sent back and forth, and the Ku Kluxers tried to scare the sheriff into a retreat. He refused to back down, however, and ended the negotiations by telling the Klansmen that they had to obey the law as well as other citizens.

The sheriff said there was a law against uncertain masked men who refused to divulge their identity. He would agree to the parade if the names of the masked men were furnished to him. This the Klan leaders refused to do.

The Klansmen held a council of war at which the sheriff was denounced for daring to give them orders. They decided to show the people of Lorena that they were bigger than the sheriff or the law that he represented. The chief of the Klansmen gave the order for the parade to start.

With a posse of citizens and deputies, Sheriff Buchanan met the parade at the intersection of the main streets. Thousands of persons were out to witness the test of strength between the law and the Ku Klux Klan. The sheriff approached a masked Klansman who carried a fiery cross. He attempted to seize the cross. There was a shot. A bullet hit the sheriff in the right arm. A general gun fight followed and ten persons were injured. The Masked Knights hurriedly departed, carrying one of their number who was wounded.

Sheriff Buchanan is hailed as a hero in Texas by the law-abiding element. The United States needs more public officials like him—men with the courage to stand by their oaths of office.

OTHER OUTRAGES

Since the Ku Klux Klan was organized night outrages in which masked men are involved have increased to a frequency not known in the United States since the years just following the Civil War, when the original Ku Klux Klan was active in the southern states against "carpet baggers" and Negroes.

A murder was committed on June 9, 1921, at Sea Breeze, Fla., by masked men who said they were Ku Klux Klan. They took Thomas L. Reynolds from his bed and punched and kicked him. Then one of the masked men shot him. He died later. Official investigation failed to involve the Ku Klux Klan.

WIZARD SIMMONS DENIES

In the case of Paul and Scott in Beaumont, Tex., an organization claiming to be the Ku Klux Klan admitted under a seal that it was responsible. In many other instances the masked riders have openly boasted that they were Ku Kluxers. In other cases they have worn regalia like that of the Ku Klux. Imperial Wizard Simmons has denied that the Ku Klux is responsible for any outrages. Whether he knows what he is talking about probably will be determined only by a Congressional investigation.

Meanwhile the people of the country have the big fact on which to form their judgment—namely, that since the Ku Klux has extended its membership and influence by influencing hundreds of thousands to get down on their knees and take the oath of "white supremacy," bands of night riders who take the law into their own hands have been carrying on these disgraceful marauding "parties" with a boldness that challenges public attention.

In Daytona, Fla., H.C. Sparkman, an editor, carried on a campaign against the Ku Klux Klan. On June 12, 1921, Sparkman received by mail a threat warning him that if he did not let the Ku Klux alone the Klan would take up [69]his case and that he might be killed. In Pensacola, Fla., on July 8, 1921, a band of men wearing white robes like those of the Ku Klux Klan in their initiation ceremonies appeared at the store of Chris Lochas, a restaurant keeper, and while the chief of police was looking on gave him a written order to leave town because of certain charges. The warning was signed "K.K.K."

KU KLUX KLANSMAN KILLED

In the city of Atlanta, Ga., where the Ku Klux Klan is strongest a killing resulted from a raid by masked men on J.C. Thomas, who had a lunch room at 280-½ Decatur street. Thomas had received letters threatening him with violence unless he "let alone" a certain woman in his employ. On March 12, 1920, four men got Thomas to enter an automobile and drove him to a spot in a lonely neighborhood. There they took him from the car and told him that he was to be punished because he had not observed their warnings. When they started to strike Thomas, he took a knife from his pocket and killed Fred Thompson who was later identified as a member of the Ku Klux Klan.

The case of killing against Thomas was put before a grand jury but the jury refused to indict him. At the inquest into the death of Thompson, Homer Pitts was identified as the driver of the car in which Thomas had been kidnapped. Pitts was represented in the proceedings by Attorney W.S. Coburn. In the official list of Ku Kluxers there is a H.R. Pitts who is a kleagle at Fresno, Cal., and a W.S. Coburn who is a grand goblin with headquarters at Los Angeles, Cal.

100 OUTRAGES IN TEXAS

Texas, where the Ku Klux Klan is strong, has been the scene of nearly 100 unlawful punishments by masked men. In one case the initials "K.K.K." were branded on the [70]forehead of a negro who was horsewhipped on the charge of having been found in a white woman's room.

Something the same treatment that was given Dr. Paul was handed out to J.S. Allen, an attorney of Houston, Tex., who on April 10, 1921, was whisked from a downtown street, driven to the country and tarred and feathered. The masked men then took him back to the city and threw him out of the automobile into a crowd. He was nude except for his coat of tar and feathers.